Kan Ya Makan
It was so and it wasn't so.

HAFIZ was always interested in jewels, it was the shimmering stars in the night sky that had first set his heart on fire. Every night he would sit outside his grandparents' small hut on the edge of the old city, as his grandfather pointed to the vast shining constellations in the dark blue sky.

 "There is the great bear," Kabir would say, and not stopping at such a simple explanation, he would spin one of his fabled yarns. He told of how the great bear travels far across the heavens chasing away the jinn's and spirits that come to steal the dreams and sleep of children at night.

"And that is why when we look up at the great bear shining in the night sky, we are always reminded of the noble qualities of a kind and loving heart," spoke Kabir.

And so, it would go on, night after night, stories and fables were told, just as the stars were endless and forever moving on their ancient journey across the velvet sky.

In the late afternoon his mother and father would come home from work and sit with them around the fire, sharing their stories of all the different people they had met in the bazaar. Hafiz and his sisters loved to hear the stories of travelers from far off lands and the weird and wonderful treasures they would bring to sell on the dusty streets.

They would hear about princes and paupers, nobles and sorcerers, of man-eating lions and the thunder of elephants. Of how many pearls had been traded for rubies and of the shimmering silks and gold that had sailed on great ships, from faraway lands and dreamlike empires.

And when dusk fell, and the city had settled to eat and pray, Hafiz would sit with his sisters and listen to his grandfather's tales.

Watching the sparks of the fire, Kabir's deep and ancient voice would take them far from the troubles of the world as they listened to the most likely, yet unlikely tales of wonder and awe.

Where poetry and eloquence brewed together such tales of magic that even the jinn would gather to listen amongst the shadows, to hear what happened next in this story amongst stories that seemed to have no end.

Only when their eyes and ears were no longer alert and too tired to wonder, and the night had wrapped them in its deep dark mystery, their Grandmother would gather them up one by one and tuck them into bed.

And as they fell into their silent sleep, she would pray to the beloved that they may sail freely through that ship of midnight, where only dreams beckoned, and the great mystery of sleep had her way.

And so, it continued day after day, the joy and tears of childhood, the scents of spring, the glare of summer, the breeze of autumn and shadows of winter swirling in their endless cycle of life and death.

All of them wishing that it would never end, yet somehow knowing it would. Just like in all stories and myths, from one far corner of the world to the other, tragedy struck where no fortune-tellers or seers could see. Such were the unknown mysteries of life and its eternal contract with death, that one thing always leads to another as the cycle continues in a seemingly endless dance.

Hafiz was just six years old, when his parents passed into that great mystery, we call Death. It was a tragic day for many in the old city, not just for Hafiz and his sisters, for it was the day when the whole earth trembled and quivered under their feet.

His parents were merchants and had been at the bazaar, working hard making and selling a few amulets and bracelets, just like they had always done, ever since anyone could remember.

Since the medina walls were high and uneven, they fell like sandcastles when the earth started to shake upon so many startled souls.

They never really stood a chance. So many people passed away that morning and the hearts of the people were heavy with grief for after that fateful day.

It felt as if it was the end of the world, and for many it was, as if the heavens had fallen from the sky, and the earth had swallowed them whole.

Hafiz and his sisters had been staying with their grandparents, eating apricots and dates in the palace gardens, playing in the summer sun.

As they were out in the open, no walls or buildings fell upon them, and so they were saved, or so it would seem. One thing was for sure, things would never be the same.

Hafiz was heartbroken, he loved his parents and for many long nights, tears fell down his young face as he dreamed all that could have been and how he might have saved them.

And so, it went on night after night, his heart heavy, shattered and broken, not able to understand why such things happened, and angry with some unknown God for taking them away

His grandparents had been so kind and offered them all they had, but they were old, and it was hard to make ends meet. So, Hafiz would go to the bazaar every day with his sisters to play music and recite the poems that his grandfather had taught him, just to scrape enough money so they could eat each day.

At times life was hard, but at least Hafiz was able to follow his heart, unlike so many people he saw struggle each day. Yet even after all that had happened, he was in his heart content, for his grandfather had given him a reason to live.

It was now many years after his parents had died and he mostly knew them by the memories and stories his grandfather would tell. These were stories that were woven in poetry and song, as this was the ancient tradition of the desert lands.

A man was not judged by wealth alone, but by his ability to open the heart through words. In this way, Kabir was a king.

Kabir was also a master baker and a fine cook and he taught Hafiz how to make the most exquisite food and bake the most beautiful breads.

He was also a great poet and Sufi master and each afternoon he would sit with Hafiz and teach him all the verses of the sacred books.

Such was his skill for learning, that before long he could remember many poems by heart.

And so, the days went by and Hafiz would knead bread and dream of faraway lands and the people that Kabir spoke of.

He imagined himself a prince, riding a train of camels across the Arabian sands, dressed in the finest silks and free as a desert hawk.

Sometimes he would imagine sailing across the wide oceans, visiting the great cities of the world and filling his ship with all their abundant treasures.

As he worked away, he would dream of the high mountains and hidden temples, where fabled saints and dervishes would gather to praise the beloved. And although he was content, there was always a deep longing in his soul.

Kabir had been unwell of late and Hafiz knew the old man would be leaving this world soon. He tried not to think of such things, for when he did, ruby like tears would fall from his eyes and splash with sorrow on the desert floor.

One full moon evening Kabir asked Hafiz if he would come with him to the bazaar, as there was something he wished to show him.

He took his grandfather's frail old hand as they walked slowly through the old streets of the city.

There was an aroma of magic in the air as people gathered for the great festivities where spring meets summer. They walked past the great temple where many pilgrims and dervishes were gathered.

Kabir turned to Hafiz,

"When I was a young man, I would come to this temple every day and sit quietly amongst the old hermits and Sufis.

One day an old man came in off the street, for all the world he looked like a beggar, his clothes torn and a wild beard dangled from some unseen chin.

They say his name was Shams and he had been the teacher of the great Mevlana, the greatest poet the world has ever seen. My beloved Hafiz, when he spoke, such words,

I swear even the gods of ancient Egypt have not heard such beauty, like fountains of heavenly wine, such spells would fall from his hidden lips.

A poetry so beautiful, it tore into my being, like a flash of lightning from the summer sky. In that moment I got to see the secrets that lay in my heart, far from the conceptual knots and chains that had bound me and entranced me until that day.

How I pray that one day you will also be given the grace to follow the path of the soul, my son, and realise the only thing that truly matters in life is finding the hidden treasure that lies within."

Hafiz walked in silence as they carried on through the city streets. He had heard what Kabir had told him and swore he would never forget his grandfather's words.

They passed through the bazaar and all its comings and goings, the swirl of life's colours and the dreams of its lovers, until they came to edge of the great western gate of the Medina.

As they looked out onto the vast desert sands, Kabir gestured Hafiz to sit and watch the setting sun.

They sat in silence as they watched the red fiery orb finally rest its weary flames from its daily pilgrimage across the deep blue sky on its eternal journey home. Kabir turned and looked at Hafiz, held his hand and smiled.

"You know Hafiz, we come into this world with nothing and leave with nothing too. Our lives are like the seasons, forever changing in the dance of life. Our birth and youth are like spring, so full of promise, blossoming into the potential of our destiny, which is like the blossoming of the summer flowers.

And later our middle and old age are like the autumn, where we gather the fruits of our wisdom to share with others, until we reach the winter, where our bodies return to the earth.

You know this life is a precious gift, it passes so quickly, like a flash of lightning in the sky. Most of all try to appreciate this gift and use this life to share the secrets of your heart and soul for the benefit of all beings. And when your time in this body comes to an end, become like the setting sun, burning with beauty and appreciation for this incredible journey.

I want you to know that I love you with all my heart and wherever your journey takes you, to trust in the great mystery of being. Don't be scared to take risks and chances in your search for truth. To find the beloved, you must have faith"

Hafiz's heart was touched by his grandfather's words and with that, they slowly walked home back through the city streets, as the stars of the night shimmered and shined like a necklace of pearls. When they reached home Kabir wished everyone good night,
and hugged them all for what seemed longer than a lifetime.

He turned to Hafiz and looked deep into his eyes, almost touching his soul. The silence and presence more powerful than any word he had ever spoken. Tears welled in Hafiz's eyes. As Kabir looked at him, he knew it was nearly time. Kabir

turned towards him, his face shining
like that setting sun.

   "You know in our ancient Sufi
tradition, when we pass from one
world to the next, we need not fear.
For us, what some call death, is
seen as our true marriage to the
beloved, that great mystery from
where we originally came.

Let me share the gift of an old poem
with you. Keep it close to your
heart and you will realise that we
will never be apart."

Do not be sad on my wedding night,
For now I shall be married to eternity
When I was hidden in the darkness of
the womb,
How could I bear this light of being?

When I stumbled into this form,
How could I have ever known,
The silk pearls of her lips,
The beauty of the beloved's embrace,
As I lay in that ocean of becoming,

And a whisper had told me,
Of the high snowy mountains,

The vast desert sands,
The kiss of the rain, the clarity of night
Would I have believed,
 Just one word spoken?

How can there be an end?
To that which has no beginning,
How can I cry to lose, that which I
never owned?

 This fear of death,
 Is it not a fear of the unknown?
 Who knows, what lies behind,
 This rose garland curtain?

Do not be sad on my wedding night,
As finally I get to meet myself.
When I spent my whole life,
 Searching for, that which has,
 Always been on my lips.

Do not wander, alone and longing.
Searching for a treasure, you have
never even lost.
A flame of love,
Has burnt this self into ashes.
In your presence, beloved,
I am no thing, yet everything.

 Do not be sad on my wedding night,

I am so happy, I can't stop these tears
The grief of knowing you,
Has taken me home,
To the centre of the heart.

Do not be sad on my wedding night,
For now, I am married to eternity".

The poem tore into the very core of
Hafiz's heart. As he hugged his
grandfather, he wept at the love that
he felt for Kabir.

Tears were rushing down his face as
he spoke to his grandfather.

"Thank you, you have given me the
greatest gift in life and that is the
gift of love".

Kabir looked at him one last time
and smiled, then without a hint of
fear or regret he closed his eyes and
passed into the great mystery as
easily as the sun sets behind the
horizon.

Initiation

Hafiz's grief fell upon him like a
wild desert storm, tearing him apart,
his heart utterly broken. Confused
and distraught, he didn't know
which way to turn, so he started
walking with no destination.

He wandered through the old city in
a daze, listening to the wail of the
mullahs, as they crowned the
marble minarets with their praises
to god. He passed through the dark
alleys with their wild aromas and
pungent smells. He walked through
the shadows in a haze, tears falling
from every cell of his body.

The streets were dark like his heart,
and he wandered on alone swaying
from side to side.
He passed the blacksmiths and the
butchers, the merchants and the
drunks watching the dancing girls
in their hazy sunken taverns.

He walked for no one knows how long, tears falling down his face, as memories of his love for Kabir tore his heart into ten thousand shards.

Finally, he rested under an old carved wooden doorway, bewildered in grief. Hafiz sat in silence, lost amongst that dark midnight of longing, whilst images of his grandfather's kind and ancient face flickered like shimmering sunlight on the ocean. He was broken and lost.

"Do not worry. All will be well, my friend," a polite voice spoke amongst the darkness. Hafiz looked up to see a handsome man dressed in the finest silk and hand spun cotton.

"Who are you?" asked Hafiz.

"My name is Namir, and who may you be?"

Hafiz managed to splutter a few words through his misty gaze of tears, letting Namir know that he was too sad to banter, yet too grief-ridden to be rude.

"Do not worry, my friend," Namir replied, "death is merely a rest place on an eternal journey. The old man gave you a gift more precious than all the money in the world and all the psalms in the bible. Do not be dismayed, my friend, you will see."

Hafiz wanted to know what he meant. How did he know about Kabir? But as he looked up, Namir was disappearing through the shadows of time. In an instant Hafiz got up and ran after him,

" Hey, stop!" he shouted. "Wait, what did you mean?"

But he didn't stop. So, Hafiz kept running after him, like the moon chases the sun.

Yet Namir was like a whispering wind, every time Hafiz caught a glimpse of him, he was gone.

Like an echo, a memory, a shimmer of light on the ocean, he ran through alleyways that seemed to go on forever.

Hafiz kept running, determined to catch this stranger, and so it went on all night, chasing the shadows, until he could run no longer.

His grief had forced him to the edge, he was tired, battered, beaten until he fell to the ground in a cocoon of exhaustion. He closed his eyes and fell deep into the dark forgetfulness of sleep.

When he awoke, Hafiz found himself in the softest and warmest bed he had ever had the fortune to lie in.
Four golden pillars engraved with the finest craftsmanship, of animals and birds adorned this most majestic temple of dreams and other pleasures.

The sheets were woven from the finest cotton in all Arabia and the blankets made of silk from the East, embroidered with exotic designs of flowers and dragons.

As he looked up at the ceiling of the room, there was a great four-pointed star set within a giant mosaic, inlayed with the finest mirrors, pearls and the tiniest of emeralds. Hafiz was struck with wonder at such majesty.

As the morning sunlight poured its golden rays through the large open window at the end of the room, he could just make out the shadow of Namir, looking out into the street, smoking a large hookah.

The pungent incense smells of burning frankincense mixed with rose tobacco filled the morning air. The music of a minstrel could be heard rising up from the bazaar, enchanting and bewildering in its beauty.

For a moment, Hafiz had to pinch himself. Was this real? Surely it had to be a dream.

And just at that moment, as if reading his very thoughts, Namir spoke,

"This whole world is a dream, my friend, everything is shimmering in between the real and the unreal, the question is, what are you dreaming?"

"Well, I seem to be dreaming of being in this beautiful room, but Where am I?" said Hafiz.

"You are at the home of the richest man in the city," said Namir, as he let out a loud laugh.

"But I thought the King was the richest man," said Hafiz.

"Ah, yes, well he is officially the richest man, but it all depends on your perspective, my friend. You see a true Sufi knows that wealth doesn't depend on material objects and bags of gold, as they are no match for the treasures in your heart. And in that respect, Prince

Aziz is the richest man I know," spoke Namir with a smile.

"A true Sufi, pray, what does that mean?" asked Hafiz.

"A Sufi is someone who lives in this world, yet has gone beyond the world at the same time. They know the secrets of their heart and are no longer caught amongst the games of this world. A Sufi has moved beyond the conceptual duality that most people take for granted.

He no longer holds onto beliefs about himself or others but perceives with a spellbinding awareness the spontaneity of each and every moment.

His mind is undivided and has no boundaries, he no longer sees himself as separate from the world, because he knows the secrets of the world. That, my friend, is a true Sufi."

Hafiz was spellbound. He knew instantly that this was what he dreamt of more than anything in this life. He was excited and scared, Namir was like no one he had met in his life before.

He had no fear in his eyes and at the same time no aggression. He had a presence that was beyond words and at the same time his heart seemed as wide as the vast open sky.

"And who is this 'Prince Aziz' that you speak of?" asked Hafiz.

"Ah, Prince Aziz. Well, once he was the richest man in the land. He had everything a man could ask for, money, health and a whole kingdom to inherent.

But that was until he gave it all away, and now he just wanders like a crazed dervish from place to place, reciting poetry and singing songs to the divine.

You see, his destiny was to sing love songs to the beloved till the end of his time. Such is his devotion, he has given nearly everything up and has found a love which so many of us dream of, but so few are prepared to truly follow.

And that is why he is one of the richest men in the whole world, but also because he carries the Mukti jewel with him,".

"And what is that? I have only ever heard of such a jewel amongst my grandfather's stories.
Is it true that the great Mukti Jewel exists?" asked Hafiz.

"It is true, and I have seen it with my eyes only once, how beautiful it is. Since that day, although I have more riches than a man could ever wish.
I would give them all away to discover the secrets of that most precious gem," explained Namir.

"And why is that? What makes it so special?" replied Hafiz.

"It is the most precious jewel in the entire world, as it is believed to be a wish fulfilling jewel, which will grant your heart's desire. All the ancient cultures talk of such a gift. Imagine the possibilities," sighed Namir.

"But you already have everything you need. Look at your soft sheets and fine tobacco, your golden lamps and marble floors.
I would give everything to have such comforts for my family," answered Hafiz.

"If that is your wish, then there is no reason why it shouldn't be so. When I was your age, I also had nothing. My parent's dead, I wandered from place to place until I met my teacher, the great Baba Attar. He taught me all he knew, and now I have everything I could wish for," spoke Namir.

"The night Kabir passed, I had a dream of a beautiful jewel," said Hafiz.

"I was wandering amongst a great caravanserai and there amongst the desert sands was a shining mirror. As I wiped the dust from its surface, all I could see was the most beautiful woman I have seen, either in this world or the realm of dreams. She was holding a shimmering jewel, shining like ten thousand suns, maybe that was the jewel that you talk about."

"It may be so. All I know is that people all over the world are looking for something that fulfils them. As you can see, material wealth can be very nice, but in itself it doesn't fill that deep longing in the soul.

The jewel that I speak of points to something much deeper, more profound, but you will have to find out for yourself if you so wish."

Hafiz closed his eyes and knew that this was his destiny to find the jewel, as sure as he had ever known anything. At the same time Namir seemed to know it too, that must be why everything was happening the way it was, he thought to himself.

And just for a moment, the waves of grief that had washed over him subsided, as he saw a new chapter of his life starting to unfold.

"You know, I have been waiting for you, Hafiz. I knew this day would come. My teacher had told me that one day I must pass on all I know to the right student. I have had my eyes on you for a long time, young man. You see, Baba Attar was a great astrologer and he predicted that we would meet one day.

On the night of your birth there was an auspicious alignment of stars, not seen for many a moon, he knew a prince would be born."

"But I am no prince," replied Hafiz.

"Ha, that is not so. You see we are all born princes, it's just we don't know we are. I told you we are all dreaming. Again, like I said, what are you dreaming, my friend?"

With that Namir lit his pipe and looked out at the morning hustle of the old bazaar.

For a while Hafiz just sat there, wondering about all that had been said. What was he dreaming, and could he change his dream?

"Maybe the first step is to be aware of what I am dreaming, just like Namir said," he mused. It seemed that most people weren't even aware they were dreaming, so at least this morning, he was one step ahead.

"Now, it is time for you to learn one of the most ancient trades of all. I will teach you how to become a magi, an alchemist, a noble man and a master thief, maybe even a prince of thieves, because I am already the king." And with that Namir laughed out loud, his face lighting up with joy.

"A magi and an alchemist, please, but a thief, surely that is wrong? Thieves take what is not theirs to take," exclaimed Hafiz.

"That is both true and false young man, but I am here to take you far beyond ideas of right and wrong. You see, an alchemist transforms lead into gold, a magi transforms the unconscious to the conscious and a good thief takes from the greedy and gives to the poor. Pray, tell me what truly belongs to you?

When man came into this world did, he truly own anything? How did all the Kings and Queens of this world get rich, the chiefs and nobility?

They learnt this ancient trade a very long time ago and made laws to protect themselves, so they could keep their power by owning and controlling the resources of this abundant earth.

But do not worry for now, I will explain to you everything in good time. It is not my intention to harm anyone.

All I care for is that people awaken from the dream they have taken for real, then and only then will they be truly free. Oh, and by the way, you know what Namir means don't you? The panther, I am only living up to my name"

And with that Namir took a toke from his smoking pipe and closed his eyes, like an ancient cat, utterly satisfied with life as it is.

Hafiz was surprised at what Namir had said. He had never thought of how money and property had come to belong to certain people the way Namir had described.

He often wondered why the world seemed unfair, why some people had so much wealth, whilst others worked and scraped by for just enough food or drink. But just for the moment he felt his body start to relax and enjoy his new home.

Namir reminded him of his grandfather in many ways, he was kind and wise, but he also had a presence that was confident without being arrogant. He was glad to have met such a man, yet at the same time he was a little nervous.

Everything did seem like a dream, just as Namir had said.

The Trials

For the next few months, Hafiz
spent every waking moment with
Namir, learning everything there is
to know about alchemy, magic and
the secret way. Occasionally, he
would see his sisters and
grandmother, but mostly they were
happy that he was keeping out of
trouble, or so they thought.

One evening, Namir invited Hafiz
to sit by the fire.

"You see, young man, throughout
history, land and whole countries
have been stolen from people.
Powerful chiefs and kings invaded
other kingdoms and took what they
wanted often killing and enslaving
millions along the way.
Many of the most powerful people
in the world are born into wealthy

families that control land. The resources from those lands they sell for a profit, becoming richer and more powerful with each generation.

These families then control the finances and the flow of money, thereby controlling the lives of millions of people.

So many people are like slaves but just don't realise it, working every day to get enough money for food, or to pay off loans so they can own tiny pieces of land, which in truth doesn't really belong to anyone.

Most of the world's wealth is shared by a very small percentage of people, that's why it is my duty to share wisdom, as it is harder to control, and its potential offers the greatest gift, which is to help people be free."

"But it all seems so unfair," exclaimed Hafiz.

"It is greed that has caused so many wars in the world. The desire to control people and land has caused so much suffering.

In truth we are already rich beyond our wildest dreams, this earth is a playground for all life to share. There are no real boundaries in the natural world, but they were born out of mankind's perception of separation."

Namir had learnt all this from his master and had sworn from that day he would play the game by his own rules. For Namir, being a master thief was an opportunity to create balance.

He only ever stole from those that had taken from the weak and vulnerable, and whatever he took, he would share with others who needed it most.

Yet most of all he would share wisdom, for through understanding, people can become free without the need to control others.

When Hafiz heard these words, he understood something he had somehow always known. For the longing that lay in his heart wasn't for more things, but to be free.

He slowly felt the shackles of constraint fall away from his heart and started to see the world through new eyes, he felt refreshed.

Namir taught Hafiz to be aware and compassionate, to use his powers of intuition, but most of all to trust himself.

First of all, he taught him to be at ease with himself, to be comfortable being alone, to learn to listen beyond the thinking mind and hear the secrets of the heart.

Hafiz was taught how to dress for the right occasion, how to be noble or meek, how to blend into a crowd or stand out when appropriate.

He taught him the secret arts of invisibility, of the alchemy of transformation and how to be patient, to become one with silence and understand the language of dreams.

Hafiz learned that the sacred couldn't be found by empty prayers and rituals, but only by creating a love affair with life.

For Namir, the labels that humans called the divine, whether god or goddess, made no difference to him, they were but names trying to describe the great mystery.

"You know, in the ancient tradition we choose to call this mystery The Beloved, and for us to meet and commune with

The Beloved was the greatest gift that life had to offer," spoke Namir.

He taught him how music and poetry were powerful ways to connect with the beloved and by losing one's self in that ecstatic union, then one would truly see the richness that lies inside everyone's heart.

And so, each day Hafiz started to see the world in a different way. He started to see that life itself was a wonderful gift and now he began to see the first glimmers of the secrets of the wish fulfilling jewel.

"So far, you have learnt well, my boy, and now the time has come for you to undertake your first task. Tonight, we have been invited to the grand palace for the summer ball.

Whilst we are there, I want you to help me gather some of the gold that was taken from the poor by means of taxes," explained Namir.

"But I don't understand why you would be invited to such a gathering?" asked Hafiz.

"Most people have no idea of who I am, for people see what they want to see. Some see me as an art collector who has made his money from selling fine works of art.

 Others see me as a great Alchemist, others an Astrologer, yet others as a Magi, and only a very few see me as a Sufi. But for me, I am none and all of these. For these are the masks I choose to wear in the world. The irony is that everyone is wearing some mask or other, yet most don't even realise they are wearing one.

They are so identified with their beliefs of who they think they are. So, from now on, I want you to wear the mask as my young nephew, who has come to learn my trade from me, which actually isn't so far from the truth," he laughed.

    That night, they dressed in their finest clothes and arrived at the palace in good time. They were ushered in to the most wondrous room Hafiz had ever set his eyes upon. There were chandeliers of diamond lights almost dripping from the huge ornate ceiling.

On the tables were foods from all over the empire, covered with the finest flowers in the most bewildering displays of abundance. Men and women were dressed in their finest attire, with rubies and pearls shimmering amongst the candlelight of the palace walls.

In Hafiz's mind he felt like an imposter, that a boy from such a humble background didn't belong in such a place.

Namir looked over at him and whispered in his ear.

"Listen son, do not have any doubt of your nobility, it's all a matter of choice, you belong here as much as anyone else, under the gaze of the beloved, all life is equal.

Yes, people try to feel higher, more powerful and above others, but do not fall for such foolery, it has nothing to do with you. I have told you, you are a prince, now take my word for it and trust what I tell you, be both noble and at ease, care free and dignified, otherwise you will never become a master."

Hafiz was shocked, Namir seemed to be able to read his mind, there was nothing he could think or do without Namir knowing.

But in his heart, he knew he spoke the truth, he had as much right as anyone else to feel confident, to share amongst the riches of the world. And with that he relaxed and started to trust himself again.

For most of the evening he silently watched the way people held themselves, how they interacted and the way they spoke to each other.

For Hafiz this was a whole new world, as he listened to stories from beyond the desert lands. He heard of huge ships that sailed to the edge of the world, where temples were made of gold and wild forests stretched as far as the eye can see.

He heard of strange lands where there were mountains that almost touched the clouds and monks lived in monasteries learning the secrets of immortality.

He learnt of great empires, where the land was green like emeralds and of great cities of untold wealth.

He heard tales of warfare and bravery and of princesses and princes. His mind drifted off with these evocative tales of wonder, and he dreamt for a moment of all the world had to offer and wondered if he himself might one day travel across the oceans.

As the night went on, the guests ate more food and drank more wine. He stood by Namir, chatting politely whenever he was asked a question, never giving too much away. Just before midnight Namir came over and took Hafiz to one side.

"Now is our chance, follow me."

On his way, Namir grabbed a coat and a hat from one of the stands and stepped outside. They walked quietly around the side of the palace until they were standing under a small round window.

"Up there in that room is where they keep the gold from the taxes. I heard one of the ministers boasting of how much they had taken this autumn. At the moment everyone is rather drunk and so relaxed, and only one guard is on duty."

Namir grabbed a huge branch from one of the trees in the garden and cut it loose with his knife.

He tied the hat to the top of the make shift pole and wrapped the coat around it, so it looked like a person in the darkness.

"Now, I want you to lift this pole up to the window after the count of one hundred. In the meantime, I will go and pretend to use the bathroom, as soon as you hear a shot, drop the pole, grab the hat and coat, and meet me by the great cypress tree behind the palace.

And remember, be quiet, be confident and all will be well."

Hafiz did as he was told as Namir rushed off. He counted to one hundred and slowly started to lift the pole to the window, hidden amongst the bushes, making sure that no one was watching.

Meanwhile the guard was sitting in the room where the taxes were kept, wishing he was downstairs, chatting to the fine ladies that looked so splendid in their evening dress.

Suddenly, a noise pulled him out of his meandering and he looked towards the window. The night was dark, but he could just make out a figure of a man, obviously trying to get in and steal the King's money.

"Ha, you fool," he thought to himself. "Who would have thought a thief would be so stupid as to try and steal from the king on such a night?

Now, I have him, and the king will make me head of the guards if I get rid of the pest once and for all."
And with that he took aim and fired.

Immediately, he ran downstairs to claim the body, shouting along the way. "Now we have him. The master thief is dead! Long live the king!"

As soon as he heard the shot, Hafiz dropped the pole, grabbed the hat and coat, and ran as fast as the wind to the cypress tree.

Namir also heard the shot, he stepped out of the bathroom, just in time to see the back of the guard hurtling down the stairs.

As quick as a flash, he entered the room where the gold coins were stashed and filled a sack as fast as he could, but only took an amount that wouldn't be noticed immediately.

Straight away he went back to the bathroom and dropped the sack out of the window to the back of the palace.

He then stepped out of the bathroom, to find out what all the commotion was about. There was a crowd standing outside to the right of the palace near the small round window.

The guard was frantically searching amongst the bushes for the body of the thief.

Like a silent fox, Namir quietly walked around to the back of the palace, picked up the bag and soon arrived at the cypress tree.

They both then climbed over the wall and before long were safely at home with the bag of gold coins.

Back at the palace, the guard was looking dejected, standing amongst the bushes with a gun in his hand with no sign of any master thief, any blood or of any person at all.

"Your guard has obviously had too much to drink!" someone shouted, and with that the party continued and no one knew any better, that night at least.

"So, what did you learn this evening?" asked Namir, after they had arrived safely at home. Hafiz thought for a moment and replied,

"Well, I could say I learnt a clever trick, and in a way, I did, but I also learnt something much more useful. I learnt that everyone is trying to impress everyone else. People seem so concerned with what other people think about them.

From the stories I heard, everyone wants to be liked, to be seen to be clever, brave or wise. I saw how I felt when I entered the palace and how rotten I felt inside, as if somehow, I wasn't worthy.

But I heard what you said and realised that everyone has the right to the abundance of this world. I don't need to impress people with what I have, who I think I am or put on a mask to feel at ease with myself. I saw that many people under their masks also feel vulnerable but cover that up through the stories they tell."

"Wonderful," replied Namir.

"You know, most people can't even see that. They believe the stories they tell themselves so much that they think they *are* the stories, they believe that's who they truly are. Most people aren't even aware that they are wearing a mask, they are so convinced of their own mythology.

Soon I will help you to truly see beyond the mask and you will see you are both everything and nothing, and that is true freedom. But enough for tonight, it's late and almost dawn.

Tomorrow we have a busy day, sharing these treasures amongst those that are truly in need. Good night, young man, you have learnt well."

And with that Hafiz wished his master goodnight and set off to bed with his mind spinning like the galaxies in the night sky.

The Gift

The next day they both slept until
the late afternoon, and it wasn't
until the ruby red sun had set
behind the desert sands that Namir
came to talk with Hafiz.

"Tonight, we will travel to the
other side of the city, a far cry from
the riches and pomp of last night.
There are many hungry mouths, as
you well know, who for reasons
beyond our control, find themselves
with little in terms of possessions.

But while they don't have objects,
many of these people have more
than you can ever buy with money.

They have abundance in their
hearts. We shall go amongst them
into the city to find those that need
help, but be careful Hafiz, the King
has spies everywhere.
Keep your tongue to yourself and
your thoughts also."

They walked through the cool evening streets, their inside pockets filled with the gold coins from last night's booty. They had to be aware, so they were careful where they went and who they spoke to.

The streets were darker this side of the city and the flicker of candles shone from the small huts and houses which huddled together.

First of all, they came to a tiny hut by the edge of the desert, where the smell was putrid as the sewers were overflowing.

Local officials didn't care much for such places, and whatever money there was, it often found its way into their pockets to spend in the taverns or on the ladies of the night that frequented such places.

Namir knocked on the door. An old man peered through a small wooden hole in the door and smiled when he saw Namir, he quickly invited them in.

"Hello, old friend," said Namir. "I can't stay long. Please tell me what news is there? Who needs help most at the moment?"

"Ah Namir, I am so glad you have come. You see, there's been a terrible sickness that has spread amongst many of the youngest children. Just next door, a young woman lost a child last week and has another one who's close, you might as well start there. It's as good a place as any. She is a kind woman and will be able to tell you where else you can help. Peace be upon you my friend," said the old man.

And with that, Namir thanked him and gave him a small bag of gold coins.

They quietly knocked on the next door, a pretty young woman answered, her face was thin, and her hair straggled behind her, but her eyes shone like the stars and her smile was like the crescent moon.

"Sorry sir, if you have come from the King, I have no money I can give, please pardon me until next month."

"Do not worry, Madam, I have not come to burden you, but to see if I can help, my name is Namir and this is my young friend Hafiz."

"Please forgive me, do come in," she beckoned.

"You must be the famous Magi, to what do we owe such an honour? Please, let me get you a drink, I don't have wine or much, but I have some mint tea if you will accept."

"That is very kind, we will accept, but most of all, how are you and your family keeping? "Namir enquired.

"Oh, I do not like to burden you with my anguish, but of late it has been so very hard. My baby son died last week, and my daughter has been ill for some days now and to get medicine for her is almost impossible with the prices being asked. Yet it is the same for many, as you may be aware, the illness has spread like a desert storm and many lives have been lost.

I tried everything I could and even went to the palace gates for help, but I was brushed away, as there was a huge banquet being held and they didn't want poor people like me giving the wrong impression."

"My husband joined the king's army, so we could earn enough to get by, but I have not heard from him for over six months, I have no idea if he is either alive or dead. I have been too busy caring for my daughter to even grieve for our young son. I just hope that I can save her. That is my greatest wish."

"Well, I am not a doctor and do not have medicine with me, but I do have the means where you can purchase what you need, if that may be of help. But in exchange I want you to tell me of all the houses where the sickness has struck."

"Oh, kind sir, how can I thank you enough? I know of the houses you speak, and I will happily tell you," she said.

"And one more thing, do not tell anyone of my visit, may this be our secret, that is all I ask," spoke Namir.

"I am more than happy to keep to such a pact," she said and at that moment started to cry, both in grief for what she had lost and relief of what may still be saved.

Namir left her some gold coins, enough to keep her in medicine and food for a good few weeks.
Once he had drawn a map in his mind of all the houses that needed help, he and Hafiz thanked her and set off around the city. Like two panthers, they prowled the huddled streets, where the houses were small and almost stacked upon each other.

As they went, they dropped gold coins through doorways. It was nearly sunrise by the time their pockets were empty, and they were happy that they were.

When Hafiz got home, he was both humbled and saddened by what he had seen. In his heart he wondered why the world seemed so unfair, that some people had so much, yet others struggled each day to barely survive.

And as he lay his head down that morning, he prayed that he would one day be able to help as much as Namir. How grateful he was to have met the old Sufi.

And as his thoughts whirled around the mysterious galaxy of the mind, he fell into a deep sleep, where the dreams of the day and night got lost in some ancient remembering beyond time.

He was out in the desert, standing on a hill, looking out to the horizon. In the distance he could see something shimmering, some mysterious light that seemed to offer a promise.

Yet as he walked towards the shimmering glow, his feet kept being caught amongst the ocean of sands, and with each step he seemed to sink further and further into the desert, as it swallowed him up.

He felt helpless and the more he struggled the more he sank, drowning deeper into that desert sea.

As he was about to sink completely under the sand, he saw a woman approach, with eyes like a hawk, dark and wild, he reached out his hand to touch hers, then suddenly, he awoke.

He was back in his room, it was evening. He could hear the music rising up from the Kasbah, as he slowly remembered where and who he was.

Half asleep, he stepped out into the dusky streets and sat down at a café sipping a dark aromatic coffee as the enchanting music swam through the air of the old city's ancient streets. He closed his eyes and let his mind melt to the evocative tones of the scented night.

When he opened his eyes, there sitting opposite him was an old man wrapped in a series of multi coloured shawls, wearing a great white turban and with a face that looked as old as the desert itself.

As he looked across at the old Sufi wanderer, he suddenly found himself looking straight into his timeless presence. For a brief moment he lost his self as he gazed into the old dervish's eyes.

They were like an opening into the vastness of space and time. And as he looked up at the smiling face before him, the old man spoke these words;

Open the tavern door,

And dance with the beloved,
She's been calling your name.
 Since before you were born.

Tear down the rafters,
Of this inn you've been building.
There's only enough love
To forget your self.

Come, play with her curls,
Like Neptune's oysters,
Praying for an ocean,
On the waves of your heart.

Gather the roses, from Shiraz and
Apollo. Be prepared to burn, in this
fire of wonder. Where every star,
and unseen galaxy, catches fire,
deep in your soul.

Make way for those garlands,
Of her moonlight tears,
They're just echoes of midnight,
Making their way back home.

Go wild with your beauty,
Amongst those rose gardens,
Where no one even knows,
Your ancient name.

Take time to smile,
At that voice of reason,
Who has locked you inside,
That prison cell.

Go catch me a sunset,
So, I can tame her,
With songs of love,
That have no end.

Pray to the dawn,
Who's been kissing flowers,
Amongst meadows and sunlight,
Daring you with her wildest kiss.

Go open that door,
Of that tavern of wonder,
Where you won't ever return,
Go and open that door!

And before he had even enough
time to ask the old man his name,
he disappeared into the night. The
poetry swept into Hafiz's heart,
where it seemed like his very soul
was on fire.

For a moment all sense of
separation left, awareness seemed
to engulf him like the ocean

swallows a wave. Life felt vibrant, alive with possibility. Everything had happened so fast since Kabir had passed, yet it was like he had never gone away, appearing like magical illusions amongst poems and dreams. As he sat there finishing his delicious brew, he wondered what would happen next.

The Trickster

The next morning Namir cooked up a beautiful feast for breakfast. Fresh mint tea, pomegranates, apricots, figs, dates, apples and cashew nuts with the finest curd and honey for the first course. This was followed by warm homemade bread, the very best olive oil, freshly made hummus, tomatoes, cucumbers and fresh cheese.

The food was delicious, and Hafiz sat with his eyes closed, purring like a cat, after filling his stomach with such fine delicacies. After he had drunk some of the best Turkish coffee and smoked his morning hookah filled with the finest apple tobacco, he sat and watched the comings and goings of the bazaar from the window.

Namir was sitting flicking through an old book, as if he was looking for something. Hafiz wasn't really paying much attention. He was just happily watching people and their strange ways from the balcony.

"Ah, here it is!" exclaimed Namir all of a sudden. "I have been looking at some old maps of the palace, as I have a trial, I want you to perform before you are ready to go after the Mukti Jewel. You see, this is a very difficult challenge, so I'm going to help you the best I can, but ultimately you will have to go alone. It is the only way you can prove you are ready."

Hafiz suddenly felt quite nervous wondering what Namir had in mind, but he kept it to himself and sat quietly, waiting for Namir to reveal more of his plans.

"So, for your next test, you will have to steal one of the King's stallions. They are prized all across the kingdom and I am sure there will be a big reward if someone were to find the horse, once it was stolen and return it to the King.

Then for your biggest test so far, I want you to get hold of the great Koh I Noor jewel, as it is worth a fortune and its wealth alone will feed a whole city of hungry mouths.

It is part of a necklace the Queen likes to wear for her favourite occasions, such as royal weddings, funerals, public executions and other such pleasures;" laughed Namir.

"If you can get hold of these items then I know you will be ready for the next stage on your journey. I will give you a week and if you succeed there will be only one more task before you will be ready to go after the jewel."

Hafiz was now more than nervous. His heart sank as he realised the enormity of his task. Stealing the King's horse was one thing, but getting hold of the Koh I Noor, surely Namir had finally gone mad. Namir looked at Hafiz.

He knew he had given him a tough task, but he also knew that if Hafiz was to reach his goal he must move beyond fear and trust that all will be well.

"Here I have a map of the palace, it shows you where the stables are, and the King's bedroom. That is where you will most probably find the necklace. The Queen isn't going to let it leave her royal gaze for long. Now you best be off on your mission. Remember what I have taught you,".

Hafiz went to his room, sat for a moment and closed his eyes, he was nervous, yes, and started to wonder if all this was worthwhile.

If he was caught, he would be hanged, of that there was no doubt. Yet, as he stopped listening to fears arising in his mind, he started to feel the deep silence of his heart, praying it may help him.

And as he heard that ancient murmur of emptiness, he remembered what Kabir had said by the temple,

"Do not be scared to take risks."

Now he knew he had to trust himself more than ever.
Hafiz took off across the city just as the bazaar was opening for the evening and people were rising from their afternoon rest.

In the day the sun was too hot for people to do anything other than pursue the pleasures of sleep. He decided that first he would walk around the palace walls to get an idea of its layout.

As quiet as a fox hunting its prey, he watched where the main gates were manned, looking for the most vulnerable parts of the fortress and what time the guards changed shifts.

Before long he had worked out where the stables were and after chatting to a guard, soon found out that the King loved to go riding after breakfast. He found out that the horses would have to be taken to the King's chamber, which was quite a way from the stables, and separated from the main palace by a forest pathway. So, there and then he hatched his first plan.

Hafiz reached home just before midnight and decided to sleep by the warm embers of the fire, as he wanted to be up before the sun.

Before even the royal cockerel had woken the slumbering dogs, Hafiz was off on his way, like a shadow through the city streets.

Soon enough, he was waiting by the forest pathway, where the horses would have to pass, before even the sun had raised its fiery head.

It was common knowledge that the King didn't pay his servants well, but with so little work, what choice was there? And it was the same for the King's horsemen, the clothes they wore were patched and worn. This was all part of Hafiz's plan.

Before long, one of the King's horsemen was walking the King's horse along the forest path, grumbling to himself, as he wandered towards the King's chamber.

And just as Hafiz had suspected, his shoes were not the finest pair in the kingdom. So, Hafiz ran ahead and left one of his finest leather boots by the roadside, and the other one further along the path, out of site of the first. He then sat and waited, hidden amongst the forest trees.

The old servant was busy muttering to himself, when he came across the first leather boot.

"Well that is a fine bit of footwear, if I say so myself, but what use is one boot to anyone, but a one-legged minstrel?" and with that he chuckled to himself and carried on leading the horse to the King. Before long however, he came across the other fine boot lying on the roadside.

"Well blow me down," he said to himself, "if I'm not mistaken that is the second one of the same pair. It would take me more than a month's wages to earn enough money to buy such a pair of fine boots, I'll not miss this chance."

He would never be allowed to ride the King's horse, and the penalty would be severe, so he decided to tie the shining black stallion to a nearby tree, while he slipped back to collect the first boot. As soon as he was out of sight, as quick as a flash, Hafiz jumped up on the horse and set off as fast as he could through the forest towards the city.

He rode like the wind and made sure he avoided all the King's guards, riding through the dark alleyways, until he was safely back at Namir's courtyard stables, out of view of any prying eyes.

Namir looked down from the courtyard window and smiled. He was proud of Hafiz, he was learning well, and something in the young man reminded him of his own journey many years before.

Hafiz, meanwhile, was exhausted after the day's excitement and decided to get some rest before his next mission later that evening. He was happy that he had managed to get hold of the beautiful stallion so easily but knew the other tasks would be harder. He shut his eyes and slipped into a deep sleep.

Hafiz awoke to the sound of prayers; the Mullahs were singing their praises to God from their towered minarets. He loved to hear their evocative tones amongst the evening song. He still felt uneasy taking things from anyone, but he remembered what Namir had told him, and that he wasn't doing it purely for his own selfish reasons, but to share the wealth with others.

He saw how corruption was rife throughout the Kingdom, and although some of the nobility tried to help, the money often fell into the back pockets of corrupt officials leaving very little for the masses.

It was with this uneasiness that he sat down for dinner with Namir, who had made the most delicious tagine of wild fruits and couscous.

Namir, however, was never one to miss a trick and he sensed what was stirring in Hafiz's heart.

"I sense you feel uneasy about stealing the Koh I Noor, and I can understand why. But let me tell you a little story, it may enlighten you a little. The jewels that decorate that royal necklace came from the Sultan of Delhi. They were not given freely however and were taken when the King's army took the city and slaughtered many of the great poets and courtesans of the Mughal court.

It is said that the Jewels once belonged to the Sultan's favourite courtesan and were taken from her hand by sword rather than persuasion.

If that jewel can now be used to help people, rather than decorate someone's superior sense of self, then I feel it is worthwhile. But I'll leave it up to you."

And with that Namir tucked into the fine dessert of apricots, strawberries, fresh curd and honey.

Hafiz pondered what Namir had said. He had seen the incredible wealth the King had, whilst so many of the city struggled to eat a meal each day. He thought of how his parents had struggled to feed them as children and also remembered the woman they had met who had lost her son. His heart won, he decided he would go and get the necklace.

He waited till dusk before he set out to the palace. As soon as he arrived, he saw a group of guards standing by one of the gateways and bid them good evening. As they huddled together, he heard them gossip about the King's stallion and how it had gone missing that morning.

Hafiz joined their conversation, saying he had seen such a horse, with a masked rider, just ten minutes ago riding outside the eastern gate heading towards the Newari Oasis.

The news spread like wildfire. All of a sudden there was chaos amongst the guards, each one wanted to be the first to return the horse to the King.

Just as Namir had prophesied, the King had offered a huge reward of gold coins. So keen was the King on his horses, he would promise almost anything. As the guards continued arguing amongst each other, Hafiz saw his opportunity and sneaked in through the palace gates.

He walked up through the shadowy palace gardens until he was just below the King's chamber. It wasn't long before news had reached the King himself, and just as he expected the King decided to go and join the hunt for his beloved stallion.

Partly, he guessed, because he wanted to catch the culprit, and partly because he didn't want to give away any of his precious gold coins.

If there was one thing the King didn't like it was giving away gold.

Hafiz waited for the King to leave the palace and just made out his shadow as he rushed past with a host of guards all following his every whim and command. Hafiz could never understand why people supported such tyrants.

As silent as a jaguar, he sneaked into the palace making his way up the marble stairs. As he peeked around the corner, he could see a guard half asleep outside the King's chamber. At once he threw a pebble to the far side of the corridor, which clanged its way down the stairs on the other side.

The guard rushed over to see what the noise was and rushed down the stairs and out of sight.

Immediately, Hafiz opened the King's door and quietly slipped into the royal chamber. Inside it was dark, just the shadow of the moon's light flickering through the half-opened window. He could just make out the Queen's shape in the huge four poster bed. She stirred a little, but quietly fell back into her royal sleep. As quiet as a mouse, Hafiz looked everywhere but couldn't find the jeweled necklace.

What he did find however was a locked drawer, where he suspected the jewels were kept. Not able to find the key, he crept closer to the bed. Seeing the Queen's beauty, temptation almost begged him to kiss her.

He watched his mind and smiled, he was not that stupid and almost laughed at the mind's games and what trouble they can cause. What he did see however was a small golden key on a silver necklace around her neck.

"That must be the key to the jewels," he thought to himself, and taking a deep breath he started to untie the necklace from around her neck. Suddenly the Queen started to murmur, half asleep between the dreams that the night can bring.

"My darling, I was dreaming that someone stole my favourite jewel," she said, and with that seemed to fall back to sleep.

Hafiz's heart was beating like a drum, as he finally managed to loosen the clasp and take the key from her neck.

He silently crept to the drawer and opened it to see the most beautiful jewel he had ever seen, shining amongst the moon's mysterious light.

He knew at once it was the famous Koh I Noor, such was its majesty.

He slipped it in his pocket and quietly climbed through the window, making his way as, agile as a monkey, down the palace walls, until he was in the gardens amongst the shadows of night.

Before long he had made his way over the walls, until he was safely amongst the city streets, hidden amongst the rabble of drunkards and merchants leaving the dusky taverns.

Enchantment

The King arrived back at the palace like a wild storm, angered to have spent the whole night searching for his beloved stallion to no avail. Yet this was only the beginning of his anger, as when he lay down next to his beloved Queen, he noticed that the small golden key was missing.

Like a raging bull he headed straight for the drawer where he kept the precious jewel, only to find that it had also been taken. The King let out an almighty shout, which woke his wife, his ministers and most of the palace with its intensity.

In a moment of crazed haste, he decreed that whoever found his most precious jewel and stallion would receive a sack of gold, two of his finest horses and enough food for a year.

Of course, the news spread around the whole city like the wind and before long everyone seemed to be muttering and chatting about where to find the precious bounty and who could have stolen it.

Meanwhile, when Hafiz reached home, Namir was sitting by the fire playing music and singing a beautiful haunting song. Hafiz sat down beside him and closed his eyes, allowing the melodies and intensity of devotion to spin and curl inside every cell of his being.

Hafiz was relieved that he had managed to get hold of the precious jewel but was also nervous that the King's men may come and find them, as they would surely soon be searching from house to house.

Namir, on the other hand, never strayed for a moment from his music and paid little attention to either Hafiz or the mutterings of the street below as he lost himself in his longing. Finally, he looked over at Hafiz and smiled, saying, "Do not worry my friend, you have done well. All is perfect, as it always has been, all is well."

The King's soldiers were everywhere it seemed, searching high and low across the city, just as Hafiz had feared. Soon enough a great pounding came upon Namir's door.

Namir got up without a care in the world and went downstairs to answer the call. Outside stood a group of soldiers who had been sent to search every house in the city. Namir welcomed them and invited them upstairs.

"I am sorry sir, we are to search every house in the city with no exceptions," said the captain of the search party, slightly embarrassed that he would have to search even the home of such a well-respected and noble man. Namir looked at them with a deep kindness and intensity, fully present and awake to everything that was happening.

"Please have some rose tea, "he said. "You must be exhausted from your roaming across the city. Tell me more of what has happened, and I'll see if I can help."

Soon enough the entire group was sitting by the fire, telling them all about a great thief who had come and stolen the king's prized jewels.

Namir listened intently to what the captain was saying, and before long had managed to hear the whole story of the captain's life and every other man in the room, all their woes, their insecurities and fears, their sadness and grief.

As they sat, he seemed to be weaving some kind of magical web, almost hypnotising each one of them as he listened to their stories.

Time somehow slipped from their memories as they drank more tea and relaxed deeper and deeper into the moment. When they all had finished and were fully at ease,

Namir suggested that he would help them to find the King's treasures and persuaded them that the King would reward them well.

By now they trusted and respected Namir, for no one they had ever met had given such time to listen so deeply to the stories of their lives. They were all so spellbound by his clarity and his reassuring presence, that before long they were all sitting together making a plan on how they could find the King's bounty.

Namir was renowned as a great astrologer, so he decided that he would consult the charts to see if they could help with their task. The soldiers gathered round, eager to see if the heavens would be able to help.

The soldiers were both scared and in awe of such mysterious arts as astrology and divination, and would never choose to argue with the gods, so each of them sat around praying and muttering various mantras intensely waiting for Namir's predictions.

Namir pulled out an old wooden chest which was full ancient charts and maps.

On each were sketched all kinds of mystical and mysterious symbols. The group of soldiers looked on in bewilderment, a little unnerved at Namir's seemingly endless knowledge.

For a while he sat and read the charts, like a ship's captain navigates the great oceans, he sat in silence and waited for the right moment to set sail his plan.

"The moon is dark this evening," muttered Namir, "and I have seen that there is a very auspicious alignment in the skies.

The charts show that we should station a group of men just outside the North, East and Southern gates of the city in the dark of night. Myself and my young nephew Hafiz, will go to the western gate where we will set a trap for the thief.

I want the rest of you to keep your eyes and ears sharp and clear. If all goes to plan, we will share the Kings reward, but I make one condition if we succeed."

"And what is that?" asked the nervy Captain.

"If we receive any reward, we will share half with the poor and needy, and it will be your job to honour that.

I have seen from the charts that if we do not share these offerings from our reward, then a great disaster will come upon each one of you."

The superstitious soldiers were in no mood to argue with such a prophecy and quickly agreed with Namir's plans. If there was one thing, they were scared of even more than the King, that was magic.

"We must also swear to keep all this a secret, and no one must hear of this meeting, as the gods' ways are mysterious and unknown, we must obey the way of the stars and keep our hearts and minds clear."

Everyone was in agreement, and so they decided who would go where and at what time.
The men were too in awe of Namir to be rude and to ask to search his house after he had been so kind to help them, that would be out of the question.

The soldiers were both excited and scared, as they wished each other well and set off on their mission to catch the great thief.

Hafiz sat and watched the whole scene before him and saw how the

power of Namir's presence had
such a powerful impact on the men.

How each of them longed to be
seen, beyond the mere face value of
appearances, for a chance to express
themselves and to be understood
and appreciated.

He saw how Namir had entranced
them with prophecies and magic,
and that they were too scared to
question such things.

Whether what Namir said was true
or not, didn't really matter, he had
saved the house from being
searched and that itself was a great
relief for Hafiz.

Every moment he spent with Namir
he learnt something new, his warm
heart and clarity were like
enchanting spells, yet mesmerizing
in their simplicity.

Once the coast was clear and the
soldiers had left the building, Namir
turned to Hafiz and asked to see the
famous Koh I Noor.

Hafiz brought out the beautiful jewel from his inside pocket, as both of them stared in wonder at its shimmering beauty.

It was the biggest and brightest jewel either of them had ever seen. Its myriad colors shining amongst the sun's rays.

"Just imagine," said Namir, "if this jewel is so awe inspiring, imagine what the Mukti jewel must be like. It will be a shame to have to return such a beauty to the King, but at least many mouths will be fed."

"And what is the plan?" asked Hafiz.

"Good question, young sir. I was going to ask you the same question," and with that Namir looked at Hafiz and roared with laughter.

It wasn't until the last of the tavern dwellers had swayed and tip toed across the dusky streets, that they set off from Namir's house.

Namir led two horses, both the King's stallion, which was hidden under glittering shawls and blankets, and his own favourite horse, which was reputed to be the fastest in the whole kingdom.

The streets were quiet and Namir knew them like the back of his hand. They slowly and surely swept through the dark and silent passageways where they were sure not to be seen.

Just in case, Hafiz would act as a lookout and walked a few paces ahead, checking each corner was safe before them. Now and again they would come across some of the King's men.

Each time Hafiz would go and speak to them, asking for a light or the directions to some destination or other. As Hafiz kept them occupied,

Namir would lead the horses past any prying eyes in the distance.

They finally reached the western gate when the moon was at her darkest and the only light was the vast Milky Way shining in the night sky.

They rode around the edge of the city first of all, very slowly, keeping to the edge of the desert's darkness.

Soon enough they were near to the northern gate and Namir made sure they were near enough for the guards stationed there to hear them, but not see them clearly.

Sure enough, the guards had kept to their promise and instead of their usual passion for drinking and gambling at such an hour, they had kept clear and aware enough to just make out a passing figure in the distance.

As Namir had hoped, they started to give chase. Namir rode the king's stallion and Hafiz rode Namir's golden horse.

They went like the wind and no matter how hard the soldiers tried they couldn't catch either a glimpse or a hair of the noble steeds.

They moved around the city like a whirlwind, soon passing the eastern gate, where the soldiers also heard the galloping of hooves and the whispering of the wind. They too gave chase, but still to no avail.

Before long they passed the southern gate and now all the soldiers that had met Namir just that afternoon was busy giving chase.

The soldiers were always a few hundred hooves away, which gave Namir enough time to put the last part of his plan in to action.

First of all, he placed the great jewel inside a bag around the neck of the stallion and then rode close as he could to Hafiz.

When the time was right, he used all his skills and jumped onto his own horse with Hafiz, leaving the stallion to run alone.

As fast as the wind they rode back to the northern gate, entering the city gate, before dismantling and walking back through the darkened streets as quickly and as quietly as they came.

Meanwhile, the soldiers had caught up with the King's stallion and were overjoyed to find the horse well and healthy as well as the Koh I Noor jewel.

That they never found the thief was of no real importance, they could only think of the treasure the king had promised.

That very night they rode straight to the King's palace where they were met with great cheers and joy.

And so, it was that the King went to bed with both a smile and a scowl that evening. A smile as he had recovered his beautiful stallion and the Queen was happy again to see her most precious jewel, and a scowl as he had to give away a whole sack of gold and other treasures.

The soldiers were happy as they were richer than they could have ever imagined, and as they promised they shared the bounty with the poorest souls of the city.

In fact, many decided to give up being soldiers and fighting for the king and used their new-found wealth to help the poor they had met and been humbled by through their fate.

As they sat by the fire, Namir looked at Hafiz and smiled, he was happier than anyone that he had succeeded in his adventure.

No one had been harmed and they had even made sure that the King's horseman was looked after by offering him work at Namir's stables once he had been fired by the King for losing the stallion.

"I have one last task for you before it is time to go after the greatest treasure of all," said Namir.

"This will be your hardest test yet, as this has nothing to do with the so-called external world, my friend, but it is a journey within."

"In order to be truly free, my son, you need to know who you truly are. And although there are many heroes in this world who seek recognition of their fame and outer success, it all means nothing if you don't know your self. You have done well, now go and sleep, your journey is just beginning."

Divine Whispers

It was now nearly a year after Hafiz had met Namir and it was time for Hafiz to perform one last task before he would be ready to seek the Mukti jewel.

"In our ancient tradition, which goes back further than anyone can even remember, it is important to go into the wild and spend some time alone," said Namir. "You must go into the desert to face your self and any fears that still spin inside your mind. If you truly want to find freedom in this lifetime then you have to be genuine, honest and earnest, only then will the wings of grace scrape away the dust from the mirror of your mind and reveal the secrets that lie in your heart."

"But, master, I do not feel scared of anything anymore, I am ready to face anything," said Hafiz confidently.

"Ha! You fool! How can you know when you have not truly faced your self? All your life you have surrounded yourself by people and games. How often have you sat in silence, truly alone, and looked inside your heart? Only when you see through the delusions of the mind will you be ready for your final quest. Now go and get ready, we will leave at dawn," spoke Namir.

Hafiz didn't sleep so well that night as he pondered on Namir's words. Before long, it was time for the sun to greet the day, so he gathered a bag of his belongings and set off with Namir on two midnight black Arabian horses towards the vast ocean of desert.

They rode out of the city gates, soon leaving behind the echoes and whispers of people, out where only the songs of the wind brushed against the endless sand.

Off in the distance Hafiz could see a caravan of camels making its way towards the ancient shrines of Samarkand. Soon it was gone, just like everything in life, leaving no trace that it had ever existed.

They rode for hours through the intense desert heat, as the sun made its daily pilgrimage across the sky. Just before sunset they reached a rocky mound that provided a natural viewpoint to the four corners of the seemingly endless desert.

"Tonight, I will stay with you," said Namir. "And after that I shall leave you alone for three days with just enough water, that is all."

"But why?" asked Hafiz. "What is the point of this exercise? I don't really understand."

"Patience, young man. First let's set up camp for the night. We can talk under the stars."

They unpacked the Bedouin tent and made a small fire with some wood they had brought with them. Soon enough they were sat round the fire drinking mint tea and sharing bread, dates and apricots under the blanket of stars that had wrapped around them. The fire crackled and glowed, as the silence of the night caressed them in her beauty.

"You know, it is like we are thrown into life," said Namir. "Often, we are so busy catching up, learning, growing, gathering, that we never really get much of a chance to look within, to find out who we really are. We take this whole world for granted, complacently showing up each day, without ever really asking the most important questions.
Have you ever wondered what it's all about, why we are here and what's most important in life?

Once, I told you the world is like a dream, but can you see how we merely dream that we roam from place to place. In a few months, even hours even this moment will appear as a dream to you. You will dream some other dream at that time.

What you need to realise is, that it is not you who moves from dream to dream, but the dreams flow before you, and who you truly are is the immutable witness of the dream. No happening ever affects your true nature. This is the absolute truth,"

"I don't understand. What do you mean that I am the immutable witness? I have a body, thoughts, feelings, surely all these are real?" asked Hafiz.

"These are what you *take* to be you, your self, but is it not true. All these things are ever changing, moving from one moment to next, and before long becoming mere

memories in the imagination,"
spoke Namir.

"What is it that is ever present?
That's what you are here to find.
Once you shift your perception
from an identification with the body
and all that arises within, you will
start to see that awareness itself is
who you are.

The body, feelings, sensations,
memories and projections all arise
within that vast open awareness.
Awareness is the ground of being,
not the other way around. It is the
witness of the whole world and, like
a mirror, it reflects the ever-
changing patterns that arise and
cease in the waves of life. You see,
when you identify with the limits of
the body and you take that as the
only reality, then anxiety and
suffering arise.
But when you see who you truly are
then you can enjoy the vast display
of the universe as it dances its
infinite dance.

This is the great secret of the Sufi masters, the dervishes and the yogis that live in the high mountains. But at this moment this is just talk from an old foolish man, when you truly see this, then you will understand that which is beyond words.

As the great master Rumi has said:

'If you are irritated by every rub, how will your mirror be polished?

Anyone in whom the troublemaking self has died, sun and cloud obey.

If you wish to shine like day, burn up the night of self-existence.

Dissolve in the Being who is everything.'

Now is the time to sleep, my friend. The great mystery of life will be revealed at the right moment.

Do not worry, all is well. The beloved is always with you in the core of your heart, just trust, that is all."

And with that, Hafiz, rested his gaze on the vast shimmering display of jewels in the night sky. When he awoke to the rising sun, Namir had already gone on his way.

He got up and drank some water and sat under the shade of the tent. Namir had taught him to love silence and to watch his thoughts, just like a hunter watches his prey.

To be the immutable witness of all that arises without getting involved in the infinite desires and distractions of the mind.

As he first sat, he started to notice how active his mind was, always latching onto one story after another, memories and regrets of the past, dreams and worries of the future.

Yet he had been taught well, and he remembered the words of his master. To just stay still, trust and be earnest, that is most important.

And as the minutes turned into hours, he started to see all the stories that arose in his mind. His life passed before him and he saw how everything had passed by, that all that is left is this present moment. That everything else was just a memory in his mind or a projection onto the future.

In moments he felt regret, tears fell as liquid grief from his salt-lake eyes, sometimes for the words he never managed to say to his parents before they so quickly passed from this world, at others for the love he felt for his grandparents and their unbearable kindness.

And as he sat, he realised that even they were just images in his mind, and how from memories feelings arise, and feelings, like wells under the desert sands, create both joy and sadness.

Yet all the while, there was an awareness, deep and vast, like a mirror reflecting all appearances, as endless as the sky itself.

This awareness had always been with him in every moment of life, it was that which never felt old, that which had watched the whole drama of life unfold but had never been affected by the stories of life.

And soon he saw that although it had always been ever present, he had never paid this witness much attention, so compelling had the external drama been. He had never been taught to just rest in the witness and not pay so much attention to the comings and goings of the world.

It seemed that almost everyone was caught up in the story, not noticing the wonder of this Presence, this very simple awareness that is the ground of being.

He remembered the words of Namir, to stay present to that which never changes, to find that which is real and not to get caught in the display of the mind. At first it was difficult, the stories seemed so compelling, so real, so enticing.

But the longer he sat and stayed with the witness, the more the silence became like a friend. Before long a deep peace arose within him, a peace that passed the understanding of the mind, a peace that felt real and unchanging.

The day turned to night and soon the vast ocean of stars filled the horizon, yet all the while he just sat still and watched.

And as he did, the images in the mind became more and more intense, grasping for his attention, wanting to pull him into so many stories.

There were moments when he just wanted to give up on the whole journey, he doubted if there ever was a Mukti jewel and even doubted what were Namir's real intentions.

The mind seemed to play every trick to pull him back into one story after another. At moments he just wanted to forget this whole thing and go back to the hut where his grandparents had lived and live a normal life.

Yet some mysterious force inside him was pulling him towards something much deeper, much more beautiful than he could ever imagine. And so, the battle went on. One aspect of him just wanted to run away, seeming terrified of change and what that would mean. It seemed to sense that nothing would be the same, it feared death and was clinging to its very survival.

There was a moment when it seemed that the old Hafiz had won. He was ready to pack his things and run away from Namir, from the search for the jewel and this crazy way of being forever. Yet something in him knew there was no way back, so he persisted and watched. And as he did, he started to see that all his beliefs about who he thought he was, were just an intricate story to create a sense of self.

A self that wanted to feel real, feel important, that yearned for constant gratification, validation, and most of all to be in control. And as he looked deeper, he started to see through the whole elaborate game, until at last he just burst out laughing, tears falling down his cheeks as he finally let go, and in that moment, he saw through the whole elaborate story.

He knew at last that his true nature was not separate from the world and that it had never been so. He saw that the roots of suffering were in the perception of separation, and that perception created a sense of isolation and fear.

Now he no longer held any fear in his heart, as he knew that he was never separate, and never had been, from the great mystery that Kabir called The Beloved. And as the relief flooded through every cell of his being, he fell into a deep, dark, delicious sleep.

That night he dreamt he was walking through the bazaar, amongst the merchants and the drunkards, until he turned the corner and there was the most beautiful woman, he had ever set eyes upon.

Her eyes were like the Milky Way and her lips like shells, yearning for the sea. She looked at him and offered him a beautiful shining jewel, so full of light it almost blinded him.

And just as he put his hands out to take it from her, she disappeared, just as quickly as she had appeared. He took flight and searched high and low over mountains, oceans and deep forests looking for her, but she was nowhere to be found.

He lost all hope and after what seemed like an eternity, he gave up the search and found himself sitting in the very desert where he had sat all day.

As he looked down from where he was sitting, he saw a light shining through the desert sand, he started to dig and as he did the light grew stronger and stronger. Again, he glimpsed the jewel, right under where he was sitting.

He started to cry with joy and just as he was about to finally get hold of it, he woke up!

It was a cry of a hawk that woke him. The sun was just rising over the horizon and the desert was an ocean of orange in the morning light. He looked up and there was a golden bird flying high above, moving in arches and circles above his camp.

He knew immediately that this was a messenger from Namir, for he was both a shape-shifter and an alchemist, and for many years had been an expert falconer, carrying on this ancient desert art.

The dream had been intense, and it was hard to tell for a moment what was real, this waking dream or the dream of the night. Both seemed to blend into each other as seamlessly as night moves to day.

He took a flask of water and washed his face, and just as he looked up, he saw Namir's smiling face coming towards him over the small hill.

Had it really been three days and nights already? Time seemed to hold no reference any longer, everything had changed, there was no way back.

The Beloved

And so, a year and a day had passed
since that fateful first meeting with
Namir. The time had finally come
for Hafiz to go out on his own and
find the mysterious Mukti jewel.

Namir was sitting by the great stone
fireplace, smoking his hookah,
singing and muttering enchantments
into the rising flames.

Hafiz turned to Namir and asked
him a question that had been
brewing inside him since that first
dreamlike morning.

"Namir, you are without doubt the greatest thief, master of disguise, intrigue and magic in all these ancient lands, if not the world, but how is it that you have not been able to steal the wish fulfilling jewel from Prince Aziz yourself?"

Namir, looked at him with an intense gaze, like a sword of clarity cutting through veils of delusion, and almost as suddenly, he smiled and said,

"Oh son, I cannot tell you the answer to that question, as you will find out soon enough. It is your destiny to find that jewel, that is all I can say. If it were mine, then there would have been no meeting between us.

Only the great mystery of life can unfold the answer to your question, I just follow the signs and omens of this world and trust what arises before me in every moment. It is the way of the great mystery that you must now follow, that is all I know. Do not worry or question the

mysterious ways of The Beloved,
she has secrets we never even dare
to ask.

There are certain things we have no
way of knowing, no matter what
magic skills or wisdom lies in our
hearts.

That is why this great unknown
journey of life is so compelling, so
full of wonder. Now it is nearly
time for you to take to the road and
leave this house on your search for
the sacred jewel.

But first, please would you go the
tavern and fetch some of my
favourite wine from Shiraz, it's
time to celebrate and make a toast
for you becoming a Magi!"

So off Hafiz went to the hustle
and bustle of the bazaar. It was as if
the whole world had gathered for a
festival of life, such was its majesty.

Everywhere there seemed to be
something happening. There were
beggars and merchants, sailors and

soldiers, belly dancers and snake charmers.
With stalls selling every kind of delicacy from all over the kingdom. There were butchers and food sellers with every scent and smell the world has ever known, all crowned by the pungent incense burning and rising through the ancient streets.

There was the melody of music, the wail of the mullahs, the cries of dogs and the howls of children playing. There were tarot readers, astrologers and fortune tellers, palmists, acrobats, booksellers and fakirs. There were sadhus from the high mountains and Sufi dancers from the emperor's halls.

There were buffaloes and chickens, elephants and sages, bustling and swaying in an intense dance. It was a carnival for the senses, and Hafiz loved every last bit of it, abundant, bright and dark, friendly and dangerous, it was the world in all its chaotic splendor.

He wandered through the maze of streets, clearer and brighter than he had ever been.

For now, he saw it as it truly was, like a dream, forever changing, forever dancing in the whirlwind of life. He finally arrived at the old tavern door and made his way through the disheveled drunkards and exotic dancers. Here and there prostitutes smiled and winked at him, trying to catch his eye in the hope he might be willing to share a gold coin for a moment of passion.

Amongst the faded light of the tavern the music rose and swayed, as the voices cackled and sang their stories and sorrows away into the deep dark night.

He managed to squeeze his way to the counter and ordered a bottle of Namir's favourite rosé, a rare gift from the famous gardens of Shiraz.

He turned and walked back onto the street, just in time to see the golden full moon rising over the shimmering crescent of the great temple. For a moment he was captivated, here he was in the middle of the city, amongst the heartbeat of humanity and for the first time he saw its true radiant beauty.

As he looked up, his heart seemed to drop to the bottom of the deepest ocean. There before him was the most beautiful woman he had ever set his eyes upon. He seemed to have seen her before, as if some wave of remembering crashed into every cell of his being, he was almost broken by her beauty.

Her eyes were like rubies that shone from the stars, and her hair was as black as the night, shimmering like midnight in the warm dusky light.

Her skin was the color of warm olive oil and her body was like the contours of the desert at dawn. As he stopped in his tracks, he was awed by her, he was speechless and struck by a fire he had never known in his still young body.

He wanted to speak but no words would come from his dry lips, no thought came to his sky-like mind, no music came to that song that was waiting in his heart.

She looked straight at the handsome young man before her and smiled.

"Hello," she said, "my name is Mirabai and who may you be, tavern dweller?"

He could hardly splutter out his name, but at least some rendition of words seemed to fall from his lips. "I am Hafiz, and I am honored to meet you, "he seemed to say.

"Well Hafiz, it is indeed my honour too, and I hope we meet again young sir" and with that she was ushered off by her entourage of guards, who guided her fine horses and her beautiful golden carriage, through the winding barking streets.

Hafiz walked back to Namir's in a daze, hardly able to put one foot in front of the other, such was the intensity of his broken but burning heart.

He felt that he couldn't live for a moment without seeing her again. Who was she? Where did she come from? Was she real or was she just a mirage, such a ravishing beauty had surely never walked the earth?

As he walked in through the great wooden door, Namir looked at him and burst out laughing.

"You look like you've just been struck by lightning, my friend, what happened?"

So, he told Namir of his trip to the tavern and swore that he would never settle until he set his eyes upon her again.

"Ah, so you've met princess Mirabai, many have fallen in love and have been broken by such beauty, my friend, but still none have captured her heart. Maybe you will be the first, at least she spoke to you and it seems she wishes to see you again.

There is hope, but for now, enough of fabled love, you must keep clear if you are to follow your destiny and discover the secret of the great Mukti jewel."

Namir opened the wine and smiled to himself as he smelt the deep enchanting aroma of roses and sweet grapes that arose from his beloved Shiraz.
He poured the ruby gold into two large glasses and offered a toast to long life and the success of Hafiz's journey.

The taste of the wine touched every cell of Hafiz's body, opening every last layer of longing, until he could feel his body relaxing and purring as the vibrant brew intoxicated his broken heart.

Hafiz closed his eyes and smiled as he remembered the last year and the magical journey he had undertaken.

And as he sat, and his body melted into the moment, the jewel again appeared in his mind's eye, shining and shimmering like the light of ten thousand turquoise lakes.

"Where do I begin to find the fabled jewel?" he asked.

"Well, you see, my friend, every year, Prince Aziz comes to the city and conjures up an evening of music, song and sacred poetry at the great temple in the gardens of the Sultan. From dusk till dawn he sings spontaneous love songs to the beloved, as people gather from all the far corners of the kingdom to lose themselves in the bliss of devotion and longing.

For tonight is a celebration of life, as you have probably seen from your journey to the tavern. People come from far and wide to forget their sorrows and stories, for one evening at least, to praise the beloved and sings songs of longing and joy to the great mystery of being."

"And this is what magic Prince Aziz is able to muster, because he himself has lost all sense of ego, all sense of importance, like a traveler or wanderer through this world, he has let go of all grasping.
When people see this, they also long for just one taste of that freedom, to know there is something beyond the daily chores of life and all its promised treasures.

So, for one night he appears like an apparition amongst the city streets and just as quickly he disappears again.

No one knows where he goes, some say he travels high into the great Himalaya mountains and lives with saints and holy men. Some say he lives in a cave near sacred mount

Sinai, deep in the deserts of ancient Egypt.

"Still others say he has a secret palace amongst the deserts of Rajasthan, and there are some that say he has no home but travels the wilds of nature reciting poetry amongst the animals and birds of the forest.

Yet no matter who says what, you must follow him and use all the tricks and skills I have taught you to get hold of the Mukti jewel and discover its secrets."

Hafiz finished his wine, and sat looking into the flames of the fire, both excited and scared at the challenge before him.

He knew it was time for him to leave, but part of him wanted to stay in the comfort of Namir's beautiful house and forget all about the jewel and its secrets.

And as he sat there pondering his destiny, Mirabal's eyes seemed to appear amongst the flames of the fire, calling and summoning him to some unknown fate with the world.

At that very moment a great crash of drums, horns, cymbals and wails of chants passed by the window. He immediately got up from his chair and went to see what all the commotion was about.

A huge parade was passing on the street below, all following an enchanting figure disappearing into the distance towards the great temple gardens.

In that moment, he realised this must be Prince Aziz himself, the crowd following him in some timeless frenzied dance of love and longing. He turned around and Namir was looking straight at him, with a glimmer in his eye and a smile on his lips.

"It is time to go my son, you must follow your destiny with an open heart and poetry on your lips, remember all is well and there is no

way you can fail, because everything is the great game of the beloved. You have been a great friend and one day we will meet again, of that I am sure.
Now go before the night falls into day and you will have missed your chance."

With tears in his eyes, Hafiz embraced Namir and thanked him for all he had taught him and for the great love and care he had shown. And with that he turned and fled towards his fate.

Namir sat by the fire and closed his eyes, he had done all he could. Now it was up to Hafiz and the world to make their peace. Just as the great story of destiny unrolls her magic carpet and invites each one of us to sail amongst the great winds of time, Hafiz was thrown into the wild world to see what fortune would bestow.

Treasure

Hafiz stepped out into the night,
knowing his whole life was before
him like a giant sweeping sky that
stretches further than the eyes can
see. His heart was beating,
excitement filled his being as he
followed the sounds of the night on
their eternal journey home.

He rushed through the crowded
streets, tipsy and alive after the
fragrant wine had fueled his veins.
The sky was deep red, and
celebration seemed to fill the
ancient streets and candlelit taverns.
Music and wine poured freely, the
world was on fire with life and
some magic filled the air tonight.

He remembered the last evening he
had spent with Kabir and tears of
both sadness and joy fell from his
eyes. Flowers bloomed everywhere,
alive with possibility, trying their

very best to kiss the sun, and
although they would inevitably fail,
they shone with beauty anyway.

And this is how the world was this
enchanted evening, as Hafiz ran like
the wind through the narrow streets.

After what seemed barely a
moment, yet at the same time a
whole lifetime, he reached the
entrance to the golden temple.
Tonight, it seemed more beautiful
than ever, as the throng of the
crowd pushed and shoved this way
and that, enchanted by the promise
of an ecstatic union with the
beloved.

Clouds of incense filled the air
and the songs of devotion cleared
the mirror of his mind, as the flicker
of thousands of candles seemed to
burn away all fear.

The temple and its gardens were
full to the brim, children of all ages
played, cried, sang and slept
amongst the wild dance of life.

Men and women, young and old swayed to the bewildering and enchanting music.

Embraced by the chords of the oude, the deep haunting tone of the ney and the beating heart of drums, there stood Prince Aziz singing wild evocative poems, taking even the most hardened sceptic to the core of their broken heart.

So beautiful, was the music and prayers, that men, women and children started to whirl, as was the dervish way. It was as if some hidden, unknown hand had taken them and asked them to dance.

Each dancer seemed to have lost their sense of self, their identity, their pride, their knowing left them, as they whirled and spun like the great Milky Way, swirling around the heavens in an ever-pulsating prayer.

Never before had Hafiz set his eyes on such a beautiful gathering of souls. Each one seemed to have lost the need to be someone. There was a sense of oneness amongst the people that he had never before tasted.

And there, in the centre of this galaxy of souls, Price Aziz was like a composer of a beautiful play, where all the characters finally got to be the shimmering jewels which they had always meant to be, but had been too scared to shine for fear of blinding the world with their beauty.

His presence shone like the sun, as the people like planets swirled around him. Enrapturing the crowd with spontaneous poetry that swam from his lips like ancient fish swimming through the deep dark sea.

Hafiz sank to the marble floor and let his body and mind melt amongst the waves of music.
For a brief moment he forgot all about the jewel, all about Namir, and the life he had been living and let himself swim amongst this

ocean of belonging, letting the words of the poems go beyond the intellect and fill the chambers of his vast open heart.

The night tossed this way and that, rising and falling in waves of ecstasy and bliss. One moment it would feel that his heart couldn't take any more, such was the fever and passion of the music, the longing of the people and the power of the prayers and tears.

Memories came and went, he remembered Kabir, and the waves of grief seemed to overtake him, yet just as he felt he would drown in tears, a sense of over-whelming love would fill his soul and joy would melt every cell of his being.

And after what seemed an eternity he looked up, and it seemed that Prince Aziz was glowing like a phoenix rising from the ashes.

And in that moment, he saw something shining from around the Prince's neck, something so evocative, so compelling, so full of promise, he suddenly realised it was the Mukti jewel, it really did exist.

Seeing the fabled jewel for the very first time, he remembered his promise to Namir and came back to his body, much like a swallow comes home to her nest each summer. By now the sun's rays were starting to shine their first glimpse of daylight into the gardens of the great temple.

A young boy grabbed Hafiz by the hand and asked him for a few coins, as he and his family had no food, nor money to buy any.

He reached into his pockets and pulled out one of the handful of gold coins Namir had given him before he left and was happy when the young boy's face shined with delight at such a generous gift.

But, as he looked up, he realised something had changed and as he looked around him, he saw that Prince Aziz was nowhere to be seen.

He looked around desperate, he couldn't lose sight of the jewel now, how had he been so stupid. Namir had taught him that when he was hunting, he should never lose sight of his objective for even a moment.

He had to be aware like a hawk, fully present, his attention firmly on his goal. He quickly stood up, and as luck would have it, he was just in time to see the turquoise head scarf and long ochre robes of Prince Aziz leaving through the temple's gate.

It was time to go after the jewel. Off he fled, like a fox in the night, a glimmer of light dancing on the ocean, a whispering wind through the summer sky.

Hafiz was exhausted from the long night of celebration, but he knew he had to pull together all his strength, as well as the secrets and skills he had learnt from Namir, if he was to keep on the trail of the Prince.

He ran towards the eastern gate and it seemed as if all was lost as Prince Aziz had disappeared into the crowded streets like a grain of sand amongst the desert.

Suddenly he caught a glimpse of that turquoise crown, and ran as fast as he could, winding his way through the dusky alleyways.

He ran through intricate mosaic archways, crowded pathways and the old cobbled streets.
 Just managing to keep an eye on the Prince in the distance, as the chants of the mullahs filled the air to greet the morning promise.

He kept running, his heart beating faster and faster, always staying present to his goal, driving him onwards, towards a distant dream. Just when he felt he couldn't go any longer, he came to the edge of the

city, just in time to see Prince Aziz
enter an old caravanserai.

Outside was a huge entourage that
was soon to be heading along the
famous silk road. The party was
made up of almost three hundred
camels, four hundred horses,
soldiers, merchants and traders
carrying spices, silks, jewellery, and
the finest clothes and foods, all to
be sold and bargained along the
ancient trade route.

Hafiz managed to pay his way in a
caravan for the journey, making
sure he was close enough to the
Prince not to be seen.
Even though he was exhausted, he
made sure he kept his eyes open in
case the Prince decided to disappear
on route. Just after midday, the
huge entourage set off into the
desert. Hafiz exhausted, decided it
was safe enough to sleep, at least
for the moment.

Once again, his dreams were
intense, he found himself walking
amidst a desert storm, sinking

amongst the swirling desert sands. Every step forward he took he found himself sinking deeper and deeper into the desert.

Desperate, he saw his whole life passing before him like a flash of lightning in the dark of night. And just as he was about to be finally submerged by the vast sea of sand, he saw the dazzling jewel shining up amongst the night sky. He reached out to grab hold of it and a hand reached out to help him.

He looked up and there before him were the beautiful compassionate eyes of Prince Aziz, he was smiling, saying,

"All is well. All is well."

Hafiz awoke suddenly, it was the middle of the night and the stars were bright, streaming across the sky on their nightly pilgrimage home.

He remembered catching a glimpse of the shining jewel in the temple, and that was enough to set his heart on fire.

He knew why Namir had yearned for the jewel more than any other treasure on earth, as it seemed to give the owner a presence he had never experienced before.

There was something so compelling, so utterly mysterious about its majesty, words could barely describe its splendor.

He knew now was the time,

Prince Aziz was still asleep after the long night of celebrations. The caravan was still moving through the desert, so he had to be careful not to be seen by the guards.

He crept out into the night, as quiet as a desert fox, remembering all the skills Namir had taught him. Slowly and patiently he reached Prince Aziz's carriage and saw that the Prince was indeed fast asleep, a

contented smile upon his noble
face.

Hafiz moved slowly but carefully
as he worked his way through the
Prince's baggage. First, he searched
through his clothes, careful as a
jaguar stalking its prey, but he
found nothing.

Next, he searched Prince Aziz's
body, his movements so gentle and
nimble.

For a moment the Prince seemed to
stir, he stopped, his heart beating,
wondering what he would say or do
if the Prince awoke.

Prince Aziz fell back into a deep
sleep and still Hafiz searched but
the Jewel was nowhere to be found.

He searched the whole carriage,
from top to bottom, from side to
side, yet everywhere he searched,
he still had no luck.

By now he had mustered every skill
and trick he had been taught, but all

to no avail. The whole night he searched and as he did, he got more and more desperate to find that beautiful jewel.

Yet no matter what he did, it was no use, he couldn't find the jewel anywhere.
Before long the sun was beginning to rise over the golden dunes and Hafiz was tired and saddened that even after all his training, all his hard work he had failed in his task.

By now tears started to fall down his soft cheeks and he finally gave up all hope of finding the Mukti jewel. He sat opposite Prince Aziz, assigned to the fact that he had been beaten.

Just at that moment, Prince Aziz woke up from his dreamy sleep and smiled with a heart full of love and compassion.

He looked directly into the eyes of Hafiz and rather than a heart full of anger or even surprise he smiled and gestured,

"Good morning, my friend."

Hafiz was startled. Words seemed to stumble out of him.

"Good morning, my name is Hafiz and you must be wondering why I am here in your carriage. Please grant me a moment to explain. You see, I was told stories of the great Mukti jewel and wished more than anything to know its secrets. I have followed you for two days and was sure that I would be able to finally see its beauty.

But sir, wherever I have searched I have not been able to find it. Please do what you will with me, for now I have given up all hope and my heart is broken."

As he spoke these words, tears fell down his face.

"Do not be sad, young man, what you have been looking for has never been lost, it is closer than you

can ever imagine," spoke Prince
Aziz.

"Although we search high and low
in life for that which we think will
bring us happiness, it is most often
not where we think it will be.

And although we can use all our
tricks, our knowledge and wits to
try and get what we think we want,
we forget to look in the most
obvious places."

"You see, my son, the moment I
saw you in the temple, I already
knew who you were and what you
were after. As you followed me
through the streets, I was always
aware of your presence and made
sure you did not lose sight of me.

I saw that longing in your eyes and
it reminded me of my own youth
and how I also yearned to know the
secrets of life. So, when you fell
exhausted in your carriage,

I placed the jewel in your top pocket, knowing that would be the last place you would look."

And with that, Prince Aziz leaned over and pulled the great Mukti jewel from Hafiz's pocket and smiled the broadest smile, Hafiz had ever seen.
He handed the jewel to Hafiz and said,

"I believe that this is now yours."

Hafiz couldn't believe what was happening, the beautiful jewel shimmered and shined like the light of the universe.

In that moment he finally saw that it wasn't the jewel he had spent his whole life looking for, but the own light of his awareness which was ever shining inside him and inside every living being in the world.

He now knew that the light of awareness was ever shining and shimmering inside each one of us, a wish fulfilling presence that has no beginning and no end.

And as if reading his thoughts, Prince Aziz looked up at Hafiz and smiled,

"Yes, my friend, this very light of being is what all the great religions and spiritual traditions of the world are searching for, and yet it is ever present, always available in every moment of life.

It was just a matter of knowing where to look. Son, I am happy to meet such a humble young man, who was willing to give his life to find true happiness.

These days it is rare, everyone is looking for treasures outside themselves not realising that the most precious treasure of all lies inside the scattered pieces of our broken hearts."

The caravan suddenly came to a halt as they pulled into a beautiful desert oasis, surrounded by palms, figs and glimmering pools of water.

As Hafiz looked out of the carriage window, he couldn't believe his eyes.

There standing before him was Princess Mirabai, the true jewel of his heart, the one person who stirred his soul more than any other in this world.

She looked at him and smiled, with a deep knowing and a love beyond words. Prince Aziz also smiled,

"I see you have met my daughter, Mirabai."

And as his heart melted into the timeless present, his smile seemed to reach from one end of the universe to the other, as he looked into the eyes of the beloved.

And, he swore to himself that till the end of his long and eventful life, he would share this wisdom with all beings.

That evening when he sat by the fire, listening to the haunting and beautiful poetry, he looked up at the great bear in the sky and was sure it was none other than Kabir, looking down and shining upon him.

Magi

The old man loved the desert as he rode along on the most beautiful horse in the whole kingdom. Dressed in the finest robes of gold and ochre, he turned around and smiled at the scene before his eyes. He was happy with life and blessed to see the two lovers meet and begin their journey together.

It reminded him of when he too had been in love and had travelled far across the world with his beloved learning from all the great masters of that time. Yet that was another story, for another day.

He let out a loud laugh as he led the caravan onward towards the high mountain peaks and laughed to himself, singing…

"All is well. All is well"

Printed in Great Britain
by Amazon